THE RED BOOK

How the
BLACK WOMAN
can begin to achieve
FINANCIAL FREEDOM

Ricky J. Hawkins

Future Vision Publishers

Future Vision Publishers
P.O. Box 1195
Asheville, N.C. 28802

Library of Congress
Catalog Card Number 93-79549

ISBN 0-9637583-0-6

Printed in the
United States of America

Printed in United States of America

PINE HILL PRESS, INC.
Freeman, S. Dak. 57029

Dedication

To my father and mother, John and Ollie Hawkins
Yeah mom it was therapy, I guess something we all need,

AND

To Those Who Believe and Persist and Persevere
Till Deliverance.

Believe — to have a firm conviction about something: accept
    as true.
Persist — to go on stubbornly in spite of difficulties.
Persevere — to continue to exist, to keep safe, to keep from
    decaying, maintain.

Acknowledgements

I'm thankful to quite a few folks who provided assistance and encouragement when this project was an unknown infant. I'm grateful for their inspiration and taking time to read – at the time – a rough manuscript. A variety of people from different parts of the country with different viewpoints and lifestyles. Thank you; Carolyn Armstrong, Detroit; my brother, James Hawkins, Ohio; Larry Jones, L.A.; Carolyn Nelson-Lawrence, N.Y.; my cousin Debra Monk, N. Little Rock; Bobbi Smith, Texas; and those with me in the ville', Randall (Blondie) Beavers; Jene' (Lupe) Blake; George Foster; Tammy Gibson; Tonya Jeffries; Ricky Wallace.

Amy Smith-Davis, Dallas; Sharon Akins, Arkansas; and my cousins, Marilyn Hawkins-Young, Milwaukee; and Carolyn Burris, Arkansas, for their opinions on the cover. Donald Britton, Louisiana for his help in the beginning.

I'm grateful for my sister, Angela Garland, St. Louis, for her support and listening over the years; in the ville', Joan Pea and attorney George Weaver II for their insightful editorial comments and suggestions. Brian Adams for proofreading and thanks for giving tough criticism. Steve Dowty for designing the cover. The reference staff at Asheville central library for saving me foot-work. Ricky Morgan for being a true friend and putting "truth" in what many people say only as a phrase, "Brother." My brother John R. Hawkins for being. Thank you to my parents, John Henry and Ollie V. Hawkins; I am because you are. The best future to everyone.

Contents

PART 4—FREEDOM STRATEGIES
DOING POSITIVES

PART 5—FREEDOM STRATEGIES
A HIGHER LEVEL

PART 6—FREEDOM STRATEGIES
TAKE IT TO THE NEXT LEVEL

PART 7—FREEDOM STRATEGIES
LOOKING BEYOND NOW

Preface

The majority white population allows the minority white males in power to erode away the greatness of this country. Since whites are in the majority and are often more effected; although not labeled as such this is white on white crime. The term white on white crime does not benefit the minority white power structure.

In recent years the majority white population has allowed:

1. Hostile takeover of companies in the 1980's. People were laid off or the company closed down. Pension funds were stolen from. While men on Wall Street made millions. 2. Early release of white prisoners, they prey on white people as much as the Black prisoners prey on Blacks. 4. Unions were created simply because white management in many companies were not treating other white people fairly in wages and benefits or plant closings. They weren't created to help Blacks. 5. The minority white males found guilty in the Junk Bond Scandal have served little or no time, some are still rich. When the Junk Bond collasped, many working class whites lost their pension fund and life savings. 5. For years companies practiced bad management. Much later the effect started to show as Americans switched to foreign products. 6. The majority white have allowed companies to close down in the U.S and ship jobs to other countries with very cheap labor. This is allowed by the government mostly for the benefits of the minority white males who fund the political campaigns. 7. Corruption and waste is rampant in the government. 8. Excessive immigration is allowed to keep wages down and profits high. This also helps keep the races resentful of each other. The U.S. allows about 900,000 immigrants a year while politicians boast that they will create

800,000 jobs. 9. U.S. chief executives make 160 times the average pay of American employees. In Japan that figure is only 16. Often they receive these multi-million dollar salaries while the company is laying off. It's obvious they aren't getting paid for what they are doing for America. 10. Etcetera

Instead of attacking these injustices by the minority power structure the majority white population has been lead to believe (and always ready to believe) by politicians that America's current situations are caused by Civil Rights, affirmative action and the welfare system. Which in most whites mind means America's problems are caused by Black people.

The minority white male power structure know how to use Blacks as scapegoats to get what they want. Ronald Reagan had his "Welfare Queens," George Bush had his "Willie Horton and quota stance," Jesse Helms had his "affirmative action commercials," Bill Clinton to a lesser extent, had his "Sister Souljah." All were elected.

African-Americans cannot continue to wait for this system to do something for them, especially in our time of great need.

Introduction

The statistics of Black women and children living in poverty are shocking. Current statistics show that forty-five percent of welfare recipients are single Black females with sole support of their family. The income they receive is not even adequate for basic living. Single Black women are the head of households in over 60 percent of Black families.

Black children are three times more likely than whites to live in poverty. A woman is more likely to suffer financially from a divorce than a man. Many Black women are in low paying jobs that provide little, if any retirement benefits. By the year 2020, two out of five elderly women will have income less than the equivalent of $9500 in today's dollars. This figure will be worse for Black women.

Married Black women and those single with good jobs are often a job loss, illness, divorce or couple of paychecks away from poverty. You must begin to take positive action now to turn these figures around.

Whether you love to read or don't read any, this book is for any woman who wants a better life. This book is different from any ever written. It was written with the belief that financial freedom starts in the mind with one's thinking. To really get something out of it, you must read it and refer to it many times. It's like a football player learning a thick book of plays. He reads them over and over until he can automatically perform the plays on the playing field. He often has to learn a new book of plays with each new team. These athletes who often are thought of as having low intelligence suddenly can do what many Black children in school and many adults can't or won't do—read and learn. It's been said that a person who does not read is no better off than the person

ix

who cannot read. The mind must first be trained over and over to believe it's possible to achieve success. While the athlete has his motivation to learn, Black women have many more reasons to motivate them to learn—far more important reasons.

Many will absorb this book right away, while some will soak it in over time. Either way is good, but you must take it to the next level and put it to use.

We must begin to respect ourselves and each other. One without the other is nothing. No matter how much or how little you've done in life, how much you've abused yourself or been abused, whatever your lifestyle or occupation, you can improve.

Everyone wins when you become a better person: you most of all, your family and friends, your community, and your country. Yes, this is your country. No one can give it to you or take it away; it already belongs to you. A miracle change in white America's attitude about race will not make this country yours, because it already is. We have to stop believing that we are visiting someone's else home or just renting. That we need to ask our host for something because we don't know how to find it ourselves.

I could not include everything in this book. It would have been too big and less likely to be read by those women who need it the most.

I believe in The Ring Theory, that is, the natural order of everything operates in a circular pattern and is connected. Today we are in an unnatural order of abuse and destruction, that many have become comfortable with, and accept. There is also a lot of good going on, but these goods are often threatened and could become an endangered species.

Some of what is written could become controversial and may offend some people, including people I know. I don't wish to offend anyone. But I made a decision that I feel every African-American must make—that we must start to do what we believe is best for our race, not just the few people we associate with. That is the only decision that will save us.

History does not repeat itself, people repeat history. More is required of all of us. You must realize that America has never and possibly never will see any benefit in empowering us.

Working individually and together we can stop the current destructive patterns and bring about the changes we deserve — that our ancestors toiled and died for, the natural good order, our birthright.

Education is our passport to the future, for tomorrow belongs to the people who prepare for it today.

—Malcolm X

Our destiny is largely in our own hands. If we find, we shall have to seek. If we succeed in the race of life it must be by our own energies, and our own exertions. Others may clear the road, but we must go forward, or be left behind in the race of life.

If we remain poor and dependent, the riches of other men will not avail us. If we are ignorant, the intelligence of other men will do little for us. If we are foolish, the wisdom of other men will not guide us. If we are wasteful of time and money, the economy of other men will only make our destitution the more disgraceful and hurtful.

—Frederick Douglass

Our nettlesome task is to discover how to organize our strength into compelling power so that government cannot elude our demands. We must develop, from strength, a situation in which the government finds it wise and prudent to collaborate with us. It would be the height of naivete to wait passively until the administration had somehow been infused with such blessings of good will that it implores us for programs. The first course is grounded in mature realism; the other is childish fantasy.

—Martin Luther King Jr.

Yes. It's been said before, years ago.
Well?

—The Author

PART 1—
FREEDOM STRATEGIES

IN THE BEGINNING

Nothing in the world can take the place of persistence. Talent will not; nothing is more common than unsuccessful men with talent. Genius will not; unrewarded genius is almost a proverb. Education will not; the world is full of educated derelicts. Persistence and determination alone are omnipotent. The slogan 'Press On' has solved and always will solve the problems of the human race.

—Calvin Coolidge

FREEDOM STRATEGY #1

START TODAY SETTING GOALS

What did you want to be as a child? Are you that person right now? Chances are as time went on your dreams and aspirations changed. Some changed for the better and others unfortunately for the worse. As children most of us had wonderful, exciting dreams of what we would be when we grew up. But as time passed and everyday existence took the place of most of our dreams. We settled for only existing and occasional fulfillments we use as substitutes for our old dreams.

These occasional fulfillments are whatever you are doing now. They have very little to do with your original dreams to set the world on fire and do something great.

Relax and think for a moment. Combine the dreams of a child with the knowledge of an adult. I don't mean the limitations of an adult mind, the things you think you can't do. Let your thoughts run free.

Unlimited thinking is what you want.

5

Dare to write down what you would like to do with life from now on. Remember to let your thoughts roam freely. Write it clearly at this moment.

_____

_____

_____

_____

How can you get from where you are now to the path you would like the rest of your life to take? What can you do? Think.
Write it clearly.

_____

_____

_____

_____

Finally, (actually this is the beginning) write down your goals. Once again be clear and definite, not shaky. Start sentences off by saying "Start," "Finish," "I will accomplish," "My plan is," "My goal is," you get the idea.

1. _____

2. _____

3. _____

4. _____

5. _____

Make copies of your goals and put them where you will see them daily. Writing your goals eliminates the excuse of not knowing what you want to accomplish. Much like when people sign a contract, the other party can't come back and say "I meant it another way." The truth is written down.

A goal is a deal with yourself.

It bugs you when you ignore it. Everyday life causes you to put your goals aside or forget them. But they're always around on that sheet of paper you wrote on. Scorn yourself for not carrying them out. In many cases no one is to blame but yourself.

Once you ignore your goals, you start living a life of "I could have done" or "I couldn't been."

Some people comfort themselves by saying, "I'm going to make sure my kids will have a better life then mine." And then instead of providing a life of good examples filled with positive things they have accomplished, the parent provides material things. Very little is passed to the child on how to succeed in life and to make the child aware of what they will face in the future. The child has little that is passed on to them in the form of property or a business. Also they have not learned the basics for acquiring these things. The cycle goes on, almost starting from zero. Many find themselves at this point today, or a step or two away. The result is that the child often repeats the mistakes of the parent. There are examples of this all around us. Yes, there are many good exceptions. But the African race in this country can not move to the mountain top with just a few exceptions.

Well has it been said---that Negroes too often buy what they want and beg for what they need. Negroes must learn to practice systematic saving. They must also pool their economic resources through various cooperative enterprises. Such agencies as credit unions, savings and loan associations, and finance companies are needed in every Negro community. All of these are things that would serve to lift the economic level of the Negro which would in turn give him greater purchasing power. This increased purchasing power will inevitably make for better housing, better health standards, and for better educational standards.

—Martin Luther King Jr.

FREEDOM STRATEGY #2

ESTABLISH A SOLID SAVINGS PLAN

Problem: Many Black women have little money left after paying the bills and some waste their extra money on short term items.

Solution: Adjust your priorities and take note of where your money is going. Look at a long term savings plan.

1. GO ON A ONE MONTH DIET. Not a food diet, but a budget diet. Look at where your money is going, take a close look at the extras you spend money on—not just your bills. It will help if you write everything down under necessities that you must pay for and then list the other things you spend money on. The "other things" is where you will do your cutting back for exactly one month. This includes clothes, eating out, entertainment and whatever

9

you can think of that you can live without for one month. At the end of one month, if you were strict with yourself, you have the start of a sound savings plan. If you can continue this financial diet for another month or longer, go right ahead. Deposit the money and decide what part of your financial diet you can maintain over the long haul. Decide to stick to it and reap the benefits. Once you see how much you've saved, don't go reward yourself and waste part of your savings. There is nothing wrong with having a good time occasionally, but be smart about it.

2. EARN EXTRA MONEY WITH A PART TIME JOB. Make it a unbreakable law that the extra money you earn goes into a savings plan. I realize this might be hard to do for those with kids or other obligations, but it's not impossible. Drop the obligations if possible and search for a part-time job with flexible hours. Some people work 60 to 100 hours in one job to get ahead. If you're working a regular 40-hour job and can add 8 to 16 hours of extra pay, it will make a big difference in your savings plan. For example, by working only 10 extra hours a week at $6 an hour can add $60 a week to your savings plan. That's $240 a month, $2880 a year. Add this money to other savings strategies, and you can see how it adds up.

3. PUT AWAY THE CREDIT CARD. At least for awhile, so you can notice the difference in your monthly bill. Pay for things you need with cash. Credit cards encourage over spending and bills last forever. Also avoid buying anything on credit. If it's something you must have, pay for it with cash. If you buy something on time, you will pay up to 40% more for it, depending on the interest rate. Misery and those so-called "easy payments" often live on the same street.

4. OPEN AN AUTOMATIC SAVINGS ACCOUNT AT YOUR BANK. Have 10 percent of your paycheck or more transferred automatically to the savings account. This will allow you to build up an emergency fund to cover three months'

expenses. It's a safer bet if you have six months' emergency expenses. If you get a raise at work, plan on saving it ahead of time.

5. OPEN UP A MUTUAL FUND ACCOUNT. Get one that suits your level of risk. Be sure to asks questions about the fund, such as what does it invest in. Look for a no-load fund, one that doesn't require an entrance fee. You can look in the business section of USA Today in the Mutual Fund section to find out what are the best performing funds. Some have an initial investment of only $100, and go up to $2500. You can have money taken out of your paycheck automatically and deposited into a mutual fund. Some of the funds have college savings plans that you can put in your name and a child's name.

   Be very selective when choosing a fund. Because of the low interest rates on savings currently paid by banks, there are many small investors in mutual funds seeking a higher rate of return on savings. In a stock market downfall, the small investors will be hurt the most. A conservative fund might be best. Study before you invest!

6. Purchase savings bonds through your company or direct from the government. Many companies will deduct from your paycheck and buy savings bonds for you. This is a good long term plan, since you have to hold on to the bonds a number of years to get the guaranteed interest rate.

7. Some have heard a lot of these money saving suggestions before, If you followed what you heard, you're ahead of the savings game. If you're not following what you already know, you're probably losing the game but can't see it. These simple rules apply to the poor and rich. How many times have we heard of famous entertainers who made tons of money but ended up bankrupt or barely making it, simply because they didn't follow simple rules of savings and investing. From the outside they looked rich and happy, but in reality they have the same problems you have. You probably know people like this. They appear to be doing very

well and are able to give the impressions of doing well, but are close to broke. Don't make that mistake!

8. WATCH AND LISTEN TO PEOPLE. Or better yet, watch and listen to people who are doing well financially and try to copy them. Also watch and listen to people who aren't doing well financially and don't do what they do. You will find good and bad points in each group, so use common sense. You may find that the people who aren't doing well financially will try to keep you from achieving financial freedom through discouragement or name calling. While others will encourage you and try it themselves.

One of the main reasons that people from other countries (Koreans, Japanese, Chinese, etc.) are able to start up businesses is that they have a strict habit of saving money. Once the money is saved, they use it for a worthwhile purpose—starting a business, investments and so on. It's not just the parents, but the whole family.

On the other hand we have the habit of investing money in cars, clothes, jewelry and other material possessions that make a person look prosperous. We all know people that have very nice cars but stay in shotgun houses. Often we have more material possessions than the white people we work for. How many times have you heard Blacks call other Blacks cheap, stingy, and other put downs when they are trying to save money for something worthwhile, or just to get ahead.

It's like when Black kids put down other Black kids for getting good grades and being a model student. The child that is doing the putting down is considered ignorant and stupid by society. This goes double for a grown-up. Sadly, sometimes neither children nor grown-ups know this. Take a close look at yourself—hopefully this does not apply.

How many times have you or people you know wasted money on frivolous things that you really don't need or can't really afford. These things really don't improve your life or move you ahead into a secure, happy future. This is only a short term fix. You can achieve something better by setting goals and moving toward them day by day. When you give your money to other people for things that don't improve your life, you're actually helping those people reach their goals and improve their lives while you get the short-term fix. You continue to spin your wheels financially, while people take your money and grin in your face. They have a reason to be happy.

Suppose you were the person receiving someone's money for things that don't really do anything substantial for their lives. You hear people talk about the bad conditions many of their race live in and see it on T.V. Meanwhile you apply their money to something worthwhile to make your life better. What opinion would you have of the person giving you their money?

Whatever opinion you came up with is the opinion people that sell things (whites, Asians, whoever) to Black people often have of us.

This opinion, and the awareness that you now have are things that other people would rather you not think about too much, because they're afraid you might make positive changes in your life.

FREEDOM STRATEGY #3

ESTABLISH GOOD CREDIT

Problem: Bad credit or no credit.

Solution: Start with your credit report if your credit is bad or get a small loan to establish credit.

1. BAD CREDIT CAN BE FIXED. Request a copy of your credit report from a credit reporting agency. Go through it and write down everything you owe and to whom. Also make sure that bills and loans you have paid off are listed. If they aren't, have the credit agency make corrections. There are a number of ways to pay off past debts.

   Go to a bank or credit union with your credit report and explain that you want to get a loan to pay all past debts. Or you can get a loan from a relative or friend and put in writing how you propose to pay the money back. Or you can begin to pay the debts off with savings.

Before you do anything, approach the people you owe and explain that you want to pay what is owed. But you need them to reduce the amount owed. They may not agree to this, unless you have the ability to sell someone.

However they may do this since they are looking at getting some of the money back as compared to getting nothing back. You might propose they reduce the debt by half. Be flexible. Get everything in writing and after you've paid the debt, make sure it's taken off your credit report.

You also could send the appropriate department head of the company a letter with your proposal to pay your debt and ask for a reduction. Skip over people who don't have the authority to make decisions, and who are more likely to reject you. After you pay the debt off, it will stay on your credit report for awhile, but at least you are on the road to good credit and might be able to get loans in the meantime. Good credit is one of those things you don't miss until you need it, so don't wait until you need it. Start today!

2. GOOD CREDIT CAN BE ESTABLISHED. A good way to establish an excellent credit history is to go to a bank or credit union and ask for a small loan – $500 will be good. In most cases collateral or a job is needed before you can apply for the loan.

After you get the loan, deposit it in another bank. Get a loan from this same bank for $500 and deposit it in another bank. If you like you can continue on like this for another bank or two. Do not spend any of the money or carry it around! After 30 days, go to the banks and pay off your loans plus the interest. The interest should not be very much since the loan period was short. You have just established good credit.

Those prone to spend money whenever it's available should not try this.

3. CORRECT USE OF CREDIT CARDS. In the previous chapter I said put away the credit cards. But if used properly they can establish good credit. If you don't qualify for a card outright-many banks offer secured credit cards — where you deposit a sum of money and are given a card in exchange. Also department stores and gasoline companies often provide credit cards despite negative marks in a credit file. Make sure you pay your monthly balance on time to improve or build your credit history.

4. CREDIT DISCRIMINATION. Federal law prohibits a creditor from refusing credit on the grounds of race, religion, national origin, sex, marital status, age or because you receive public assistance. If you think you're a victim of credit discrimination, contact the Federal Trade Commission, Correspondence Branch, Washington, D.C. 20580.

FREEDOM STRATEGY #4

INVEST IN REAL ESTATE

Single family houses, duplexes and multi-dwelling units can all be good long term investments. Depending on your particular situation, you may want to consider buying real estate. The payment on a house with a reasonable interest rate, with taxes and insurance included, is lower or almost equal to the rent you pay on some apartments. Also you have the benefits of being able to deduct the interest on your mortgage payment and build up savings through equity.

If the house or apartments are rental units, more deductions apply. Some people pay no income taxes on their regular job income because of tax write offs on their real estate. The tax laws are tighter now, but they still present opportunities for the investor.

Programs at various banks can help people who might not ordinarily qualify for a loan. Some require only a 3 percent down payment and lower points. Consultants help on various financial problems you might have. Every program is different. Contact local banks. You can also approach an owner of a property that you are interested in buying about owner financing. There is no need to qualify with a bank or other associated costs. You still need to be careful.

You might want to consult a buyer's broker. For a fee this person will represent your interests in buying a property.

17

It's money well spent, especially if you are new to real estate investing. Don't try to save a few hundred dollars by not getting advice up front.

Read real estate books before spending. The library reference desk knows of the best books. Learning before investing cannot be stressed enough.

A major advantage to owning a duplex or triplex is that the rents you collect pays the mortgage, or most of it. You can live in the other half of the duplex for free. The money saved can be used in other investments.

Another good way to invest is to buy a house or apartment that needs minor fix-ups. You can do the work, or contract out. Many people have quit their jobs and gone into buying properties to fix-up and resell. Some keep their jobs and work in real estate part-time. Reselling is a good choice if you don't want to be a landlord.

Large and small cities have many houses and buildings suitable for fix-up. These represent great opportunities. In many cities people have returned from the suburbs and bought places in need of repair. Others follow and soon a whole area takes on a better look. This is called gentrification. It's also called "people not seeing the value of what they have, until someone takes it away." The old residents sometimes have to move elsewhere because the rents and taxes are now higher. But, it's very possible that the current residents of communities that need fixing-up can perform these changes themselves for their own good and the good of the community. It's a great feeling to see something drab transformed into something attractive and be able to say "I did that."

Ask a real estate agent about HUD homes. There are low interest loans and grants for homeowners and investors through HUD's Section-Eight program for fix-up of houses.

If you have someone going to college, away from home, buy a house or apartment and rent out to your child and other college students. You can deduct from your taxes; management fees, interest and other tax deductions. You can also deduct the costs of going to see about your property. It's a good way to reduce college costs.

FREEDOM STRATEGY #5

BUY A USED CAR INSTEAD OF A NEW ONE

"The best time to buy a new car is when you are financially secure," but some people don't even then. You often see wealthy people driving old cars. One reason is that when you make it financially and are secure, there's no need to show what you can buy. They believe it's better to drive an old car and stay in a very nice house than to drive a nice car and stay in a average place. They know a house's value increases, while a car's value decreases as soon as you drive off the car lot.

Payments and interest on something that is going down in value is money that you can never recover. Begin your search in the Consumer Reports Buying Guide Issue at the library or a bookstore. It lists the repair records of cars, you can see which car is likely to cause less trouble. If you visit the

19

library, xerox copies of cars with good repair record, this saves
you the return trips. (The Consumer Reports Buying Guide
is an excellent reference for any product you buy.)

Don't take the word of a salesman or the owner that a
car is in good condition, and don't be fooled by a car that
is clean and shiny. Have a mechanic to check it out. Let them
know you're thinking about buying the car. This should cost
less than a hundred dollars even if they hook it up to a
diagnostic computer. Price varies but it will be money wisely
spent and it will save you from a headache later. (A diagnostic
computer gives the mechanic readings on the engine – what's
wrong and what's right). If you have a trade in, you may
also want to have it checked out before you let the salesman's
mechanic look it over. You'll then be able to compare if they
say something is wrong. Also know the value of your trade in.

Before spending money to have the car checked out, have
a sale price agreed upon. Also arrange for the financing ahead
of time. This gives you a better bargaining hand since the
salesman doesn't have to worry if you will qualify for a loan,
really speeding things up.

If possible get a short term loan and make a big down
payment for a quick payoff. Or pay all cash if you wish. Get
the loan value from the bank. This is how much they will
loan you for the car. Anything paid above that will be your
downpayment, or you can pay more. Remember you have to
pay taxes, title and insurance.

The bank or credit union used car book goes back five
years. If you are buying a used car over five years old and
there are a lot of good cars that old. Call the library for the
NADA retail and wholesale value of the car. You might have
to finance with a financing agency since some banks won't
loan on older cars. It's not because they aren't good cars, but
banks work by certain guidelines.

The salesman will likely have the car at the retail price.
You want to buy the car for the wholesale price or between
the retail and wholesale price.

Don't have your heart set on a certain car if it's at the
wrong price or in poor condition. You want to be smart, not
a sucker. Have a number of cars in mind, so that you have

choices. If you make an offer and the dealer acts as if you're stealing from him, don't go any higher. Leave your number and tell the salesman to give you a call if he wants to sell the car to you. Be assertive. In the meantime, have other cars that you're interested in. You might make an offer on two or three cars in one day. Most car lots are filled with used cars, so you should have a decent choice. Also you need to remember that some cars sell faster than others. If you pick the cars with the best repair records, those are likely to be the best sellers. Don't let that worry you. There are plenty of those cars, too. But you must do your homework to know what is a good price for a car.

Don't let a car with high mileage discourage you from buying it. If the car is well taken care of and runs well, it could be a good buy. Some cars with a hundred thousand miles still can roll another hundred thousand miles with the same engine. A good older car that you can pay off quickly and drive for a hundred thousand miles is far better than a newer car that you can drive the same amount, but have to pay for over the next four to six years. Your new car will have the value of a used car long before you finish paying for it. You could be applying that money to something worthwhile.

If you decide to buy a new car; there's nothing wrong with that if you're in a position to do so. Keep in mind that a white woman pays about $150 more for a car than a white man and an African-American woman pays about $800 more for the same car. Many of the same rules apply. Don't get taken. Don't get frustrated and stay calm. Your work will be well worth the effort.

FREEDOM STRATEGY #6

THE GOOD NEWS IS,
YOU CAN MAKE A CHOICE

Question: What will hold you back more than the strongest racism?

Answer: Low self-esteem, a belief that you cannot accomplish anything on a grand scale.

THE GOOD NEWS IS, YOU CAN MAKE A CHOICE

If someone is holding you back other than yourself, there you have it! For someone to want to hold you back, they must think that you have the ability to get ahead in life and pass them by. If not, they would have no reason to attempt to keep you down.

If you were competing against a child in a game, there would not be a reason to cheat the child or discourage them

22

from winning. You know they have not developed the skills to win and mostly they will beat themselves.

The only reason for someone to try to keep you down is that you do have something of value to offer. If they think you have nothing of value to threaten them with, there is no reason to keep you down. They know you will keep your self down better than they could and with less trouble.

The good news is you must have valuable skills. You only need to focus them!

Do you feel you're holding yourself back? That's also good news. Why? Because you're in control of your destination. The choice of success in life or failure rests completely in your hands. Reading this book says you want to choose success for your life, and that's an excellent start.

You made a choice. Now make a determination.

You've lived a life not believing in yourself. Now try believing in yourself and your abilities and that you can acquire other talents. Class and style are not how much money you have, but what you think about and do. You've lived on the other side. Now it's time to move on. Say to yourself, "I will."

SOMETHING MORE POWERFUL THAN DRUGS

If you're on drugs, one reason is because you have nothing stronger than drugs that you care about. No powerful dreams or ambitions that are stronger than the drugs. I've seen many times where a person is on drugs and then someone close to them dies. Then they can drink or do drugs all day and not be drunk or high. This is because their grief is stronger than the alcohol or drugs. They are focused on their grief. Their grief is more powerful.

Some at this low point in their life decide to quit drinking and doing drugs. They hate being a Geek Monster (A cocaine and crack user). Some are successful, most stay off for awhile and then start again. What is missing is a powerful ambition—a forgotten dream or goal that will defeat the self-destructive need to drink or do drugs. The will to succeed must be equal to the powerful forces that drive a drug addict to somehow get $200 a day to service their habit. Those negative forces must be focused in a positive direction. The anger too must be focused and used to your benefit.

You must make a determination to find something more powerful than your self-inflicted abuse – something that you can be more passionate about than sex and drugs – a powerful new focus. You must search as if your life depended upon it, because it does.

If you don't care about your life, it doesn't matter if you live or die. Sit down in a quiet place and think of somebody else you would like to be. Anybody. Play make-believe for a little while. Through your imagination you now feel you have something to live for in the form of another person. At least for a short time you felt that your existence on this earth was important. You must begin to discover something in the real world that gives you the same feelings.

You are not weaker than other people. Often when white males in a position of authority gets laid off or fired from their jobs, they develop the same negative outlook on life a unsuccessful Black person may have – who has never had a position of authority or a decent chance at success. These white males have one of the highest suicide rates. Or they sometimes kill other people.

The strength, courage and wisdom of every slave woman allowing them to survive a cruel vicious life-that strength exists today in every African-American woman. Harriet Tubman after escaping slavery, returned to the south nineteen times to bring three hundred slaves North out of slavery. A huge bounty of $40,000 hung on her head. Can you imagine what would have happened to her if she was captured?

No other race of woman can match the courage and strength of Black women slaves who gave birth one night and had to get up the next morning and go right back to pickin' cotton under a scorching sun, without missing a minute's work. That toughness, bravery and caring is here today in you, it's yours. Will you claim it?

I could write pages on why you are a Queen of a person. But I won't. You must dig for those truths yourself.

Enjoy your journey.

PART 2—
FREEDOM STRATEGIES

MINDING YOUR OWN
BUSINESS

We must become mechanics; we must build as well as live in houses; we must make as well as use furniture; we must construct bridges as well as pass over them, before we can properly live or be respected by our fellow men. We need mechanics as well as ministers. We need workers in iron, clay, and leather---To live here as we ought we must fasten ourselves to our countrymen through their every day cardinal wants. We must not only be able to black boots, but to make them.

—Frederick Douglass

FREEDOM STRATEGY #7

WHAT CAN YOU DO FOR OTHERS

Think. What service can you provide for your community? I got the idea for this book from women who are struggling through life financially without knowledge of the basic skills needed to advance. And also those women who are doing okay but can't seem to get to a level of financial freedom. Often it's the thinking that needs adjustment, not the amount of money earned.

I've met women who wanted to buy a house but didn't have good credit or the down payment. They also didn't know the process of buying a house. Some wanted to rent a nice apartment but didn't have the money after paying necessary bills. These women held steady jobs. They cared about themselves and others, and desired to improve their lives and the lives of any children they had.

I asked myself "what can I do for their benefit?" That's how I came up with the idea of writing a different kind of financial help-book for Black women. After I am successful in helping Black women, this will also benefit their children and others. It's better to be successful if that success comes from helping someone else.

I should benefit in many ways, including financially. But I didn't write this book just to make money. If this book is a success, that says there are a lot of people putting forth efforts that are going to help themselves, our race and this country. Also, others will try to help people once they see positive changes. Regretfully, some will be motivated more by financial gain, than uplifting the race. You must be watchful.

What would it be like if African-Americans finally moved into a Promised Land on this earth? In these United States? The process starts in your mind.

What can you do? What product or service can you provide for your community and the global community? People are telling you their wants and needs. Think. Tap into those needs and get started.

FREEDOM STRATEGY #8

THIS TIME IT'S OKAY TO COPY

Copying was against the rules in school and can be grounds for a lawsuit if one business steals the name or patented product of another business. But this time it's okay to copy.

For years other people have copied Black music, dance, language expressions, clothes, style, hair and physical appearances. Many traditions and laws we have today were based on what was developed and established elsewhere.

Now, you want to copy the business ideas, marketing strategy, products and services of a successful company. There are two ways to get an economic share of an existing product market. Create a new untested product or make the same product as another successful company and compete for a share of their established marketplace (better known as sales to consumers or other businesses). You'll offer better service, better prices and better quality to the consumers, thus gaining a healthy market share.

Pick any good product or service and a good business. Study it from the ground up. You can purchase manuals on how to start any business. Ask the library for help. There is not much information on some businesses, so you'll have to research. Many great companies were built off the ideas and experience of other companies. You can do the same thing. It's our time. It's only fair.

31

How long? The answer is: as long as we permit it. I say that Negro action can be decisive. I say that we ourselves have the power to end the terror and to win for ourselves peace and security through land.

—Paul Robeson

FREEDOM STRATEGY #9

WHICH BUSINESS TO START?

The first choice for which business to start is one you feel passionate about, would love to do and has a better than average chance for success.

Suppose you started a business and hired Black youth and others striving to make it, your product is well made and priced according to the market (two very important things), and you advertised your company as what it was doing for the community – uplifting the race and the nation – do you think people would respond by purchasing your product?

The leaders quoted in this book believe that others would respond and need to respond. They believed this when things were just as bad as today or worse.

People know of the plight of others. They say they want to make a difference and would do the right thing, so isn't it time you took them up on that? Do you think they're just talking and won't be around when you sell your product?

I'm not against something as controversial as a brewery or distillery as a business. Many Black folks do drink (and many do not). They won't drink more or less if the alcohol is Black owned. But we can make a choice of what we drink in this country. I believe most would choose a company that is Black owned and is really trying to do something for the Black community in it's greatest time of need. I wouldn't mind if a distillery was in the middle of East St. Louis, Cabrini Green Projects in Chicago, Roxbury in Boston, the Fifth Ward in Houston or Harlem, and provided full employment for it's residents. At least it's on the way to eliminating the current situations. Strict guidelines and regulations would have to be established as in most companies. Some areas could be supported just on what is consumed in their city by other Blacks.

I'm not advocating making liquor as a business, I'm advocating new and creative solutions combined with what we have learned from the past.

(NOTE: For those who live in places with few Black Businesses, and you wish to make contact with them, call information for a large city and ask for the phone number of the Black Pages. You can then ask for information or order a copy of the Black Pages. Or look in – 'Try Us' – National Minority Business Directory at your library's reference desk.)

FREEDOM STRATEGY #10

LET'S START A BUSINESS

Black women buy loads of shoes and perfume. For some companies this provides much of the profit margin. If Black women didn't buy these products, the profits of the white-owned companies would go down, noticeably. This represents power for the Black woman. A power that's not being used or increased.

This chapter outlines procedures and thought patterns for starting a shoe or perfume company. It's not an all-consuming study, but a general guide. Your research will answer in-depth questions about your particular interest. Shoes are only an example, any product in demand will do. Think about the needs of your community, the larger African-American community and the nation. What can you do to fulfil their needs?

Let's get started on your company.

Assume that your potential customers are in your neighborhood. This is the area that your company is going

35

to service. While doing this exercise, keep your customers in mind.

A. SHOE COMPANY
   Your company's name? Write it at the top of a sheet of paper.

B. WHAT TYPE OF SHOE COMPANY
   Will you make women's dress shoes, tennis shoes, children's shoes, or create something new? Starting off, it might be best to specialize. Consider your likes and what's in demand.

C. FINANCING YOUR COMPANY
   Personal savings? A bank loan? The Small Business Administration? Loans from relatives? Business partners with money or other resources? Look at the short and long term financial future of your company. Many small businesses fail soon after start-up. What will be your start-up costs?

D. WHAT DO YOU KNOW ABOUT THE SHOE BUSINESS
   This is where your research comes in. Go to the library, visit shoe companies, and attend conventions and seminars. Write a paper. Read related magazines. Why do some companies fail while others prosper? Who is your competition? How can you be better than the competition? Visit SCORE for free business advice. (Service Corps of Retired Executives)

E. HOW WILL YOU MARKET YOUR PRODUCT
   Will you use mail order, magazine and newspaper ads, or sell door to door? Or maybe radio or T.V. will be more effective. Will an entertainer sell your product? Many Black entertainers are recognizable faces. Few are asked to market a good product, and most would welcome the chance. Exposure is their business. What provides the most return for the least money? The correct advertising can make your business, bad advertising can break it.

F. LOCATION

Do you want a home based business or will you rent office space? The shoe business needs space for equipment and employees. (This is a start-up cost.) Do you need a location where people pass by regularly?

G. EMPLOYEES

How many? Just you in beginning? What benefits, training and wages are required? What business laws regulate your business? Research, answer these questions and others you come up with.

H. PARTNERS OR GO IT ALONE

Is a partner a benefit? If you are feeling overwhelmed by the prospect of starting your own business or if you are weak in some areas of business, try to find a suitable partner. This makes your chances for success greater. Or if it's best to have only one decision maker, go it alone. There are successful companies that work both ways.

I. THE FUTURE

Where do you see yourself and your company in the future? Whatever age you are now it's a good idea to look many years ahead. You want a legacy. What changes take place in the future, good and bad? What's the effect on your company? What adjustments can you make now to come out on top? What can you do today to make the future better?

PART 3—
FREEDOM STRATEGIES

OUR FUTURE

He who starts behind in the great race of life must forever remain behind or run faster than the man in front.

—Benjamin E. Mays

FREEDOM STRATEGY #11

PROVIDE FOR A CHILD'S EDUCATION IN UNUSUAL WAYS

Many athletes go to school on football, basketball and track scholarships. Many other athletic ways exists to pay for college, that are mostly untapped. There are many colleges that provide full or partial scholarships. Since these schools may be looking for qualified Black student/athletes to participate in sports where there are very few Blacks, your child's chances for a scholarship are good. If your child is also a very good scholar, chances are better.

These sports are: golf, tennis, baseball, volleyball, swimming, gymnastics, archery, badminton, skating, wrestling, and others. Your child need not be of Olympic caliber to get a scholarship in these sports. Some of these sports have limited scholarships. Don't let that stop you from encouraging your child to pursue a sport such as archery, since there also will be less competition for a scholarship.

Research available scholarships at the library reference desk in the Peterson College Money Handbook, which is updated each year. Sit down with your child to find out what their interests are. Chances are they won't mention many of these "not-every-day" sports. Remember they need to be introduced to these sports through you or their school. Some insisting may be needed on your part. One reason children don't do anything as kids and then as adults is because they have too many choices, and no one to lead them into something and insist that they stick it out. Many successful people will tell you that they are grateful to someone in their past who wouldn't let them quit. While some resent their parents pick of their careers. Use good judgment, be flexible.

These sports may not be considered as the thing to do, though many people have seen them in the Olympics. Those that excel at the professional level make sums of money comparable to well-known sports. Blacks competing successfully at one of these lesser known sports would stand out even more, simply because there aren't many Blacks in them. Look at the short and the long term range for you and your family and see how you could benefit.

Take golf as an example. Introduce your child to golf at an amusement golf park. These are inexpensive and you don't have to know the game. Consider this an adventure and learning experience for everyone. If a friend of your child shows an interest, bring them along. This will motivate your child more. Later, they can play at the city golf course or high school. If the high school doesn't have a golf program, the child can play on their own. Many people do this.

When they are ready, they can approach a college to show their game. It's best to do this a year or two before graduating to make contacts and to get information from different schools. Remember, there are many ways to get what you want.

If after a considerable amount of time your child does not show an ability to win in competition, you should move on to another sport. Remember you're hoping your child will receive a college scholarship, not just fill time.

An inexpensive set of new golf clubs can be bought or you might check the ads to find a used set. Remember to find out what a used set of a particular brand of golf clubs should cost before negotiating for the best buy. There are summer schools for golf that your child can attend. You can find out about these from high schools, other golfers, and Country Clubs. Call the reference desk at the library or your newspaper's sports editor. Find out if grants or scholarships are available for these training schools.

What remains is for you to think, and put your plan into action.

FREEDOM STRATEGY #12

START YOUR CHILD ON A SOLID FINANCIAL FOUNDATION

Start your child on a solid financial foundation while they are growing up. If you didn't and they are now older, it's still not too late. As adults we must set good examples for saving that our children can see.

1. OPEN A BANK ACCOUNT. You and your child can open a bank account in your child's name. Encourage them to put their allowance in the bank account and let it build up. This can have a positive impact on the rest of their lives.

2. START A BUSINESS. What service for the community or product can your child provide that will turn a profit? When I was a boy, it was a paper route. Having something you're responsible for makes you a responsible person.

3. BECOME AN INVESTOR. Teach your child how to read the stock pages. If you don't know how, ask a stock broker. Your child should make their own investment decisions with your help, not a stock broker's. Look out for your own best interests.

For most of us the stocks flashing across the T.V. screen are a foreign language. You need to learn about things that people make money off of (and lose money on) and pass this on to your child. The so-called "money experts" aren't more intelligent than you. One of the biggest reasons the rich get richer is that they take a long-term view. They look past tomorrow. It's never too early to be taught this or too late.

Have the child invest savings in one stock at a time. Many banks offer discount brokerage services. Help them pick a stock that they can relate to, such as toy makers, amusement parks, sports related, etc. Later they can invest in companies solely on the basic of, if the stock will make money. They should invest after doing some form of research, even if just reading about the company in the newspaper. Many people make investment decisions based on newspaper articles. Good information will help determine if it's wise to invest in the company. This experience will open up a whole new world for your child and also for you. You can also start an investment club with family and friends.

Enter the AT & T Collegiate Investment Challenge, which is open to high school and college students. Each person starts off with a fictional $500,000 account. The top high school and college stockpicker receives $1,000 and $8,000, respectively, plus other prizes. For additional information, call 1-800-545-8808.

There is also The Stock Market Game offered by the Securities Industries Association. Student teams compete against one another. They get to invest a fictional $100,000 in stocks. The entry fee is $18. For additional information call 609-771-3288.

There are also investment games and books for kids and teenagers. Inquire at the reference desk at your library or a bookstore.

The child will begin to look beyond the final product that is on the store shelf. They will become interested in what goes on inside a company. They will begin to wonder what many top executives are doing to make more money than most people in entertainment. They will start to believe that you can make more money with your mind than with your muscles or by hustling.

4. DEVELOP WORD POWER. Have your child to define words and use them in sentences. Or call out words from a dictionary or thesaurus for them to define. The top people in business usually know how to define the most words and how to use those words. That doesn't mean they go around using big words, but they know the meaning of them.

5. KEEP A JOURNAL. This is a tool for self-discovery and self-expression. Writing whatever you feel brings the inner thoughts out, provides excellent therapy, and develops imagination and visualization. If your child is interested in hip hop music (rap), have them look at the words to songs that come with the cassettes. These were written by people just like them who have a need to express themselves. Many of the songs from activist inspired rap artists have a positive message, such as Public Enemy and Paris. I recommend Public Enemy's past and future work and Paris's cassette "Sleeping With The Enemy" to anyone. Paris's work has some curse words. The U.S. is increasingly becoming a four letter cuss word country. He is just letting you know that and what you can do about it. Look past the surface.

Journals are also good for adults. Many people tell me that they want to put their thoughts and life down on paper, but never do. They don't realize all the benefits they would receive. You also must be aware that this can open up old painful wounds. Write free style—let the words flow and don't correct anything. It's not a test.

Every few weeks make copies and place with a friend for safe keeping, in case of fire or accident to the original. What you write is valuable.

Perhaps we shall be the teachers when it is done. Out of the depths of pain we have thought to be our sole heritage in this world—O, we know about love!

And that is why I say to you that, though it be a thrilling and marvelous thing to be merely young and gifted in such times, it is doubly so, doubly dynamic—to be young, gifted and Black.

—Lorraine Hansberry

All diamonds were once a lump of coal.

—The Author

FREEDOM STRATEGY #13

TO THOSE IN HIGH SCHOOL AND COLLEGE

You have the chance to develop the skills necessary to direct your life in any direction you choose. All the mistakes as well as the victories are laid before you. Choose what you can use to your advantage.

Generally, Black students are thought of as being less intelligent than the average white students. Those that excel are thought of as being smart for their race. They are believed to be a rare find. You can excel more than anyone. The question is, will you choose to?

The job market is tough for everyone coming out of college. You know it has to be tougher for African-Americans. Our unemployment is stuck in double digits and many people are underemployed. Many have turned to the drug trade for income. Often this leads to violence and to prison, as many

50

people can attest to. Some companies will hire a few of us to offset criticism, while some won't hire any of us. There are a few companies committed to fair hiring, but far from enough. Once you're hired, sometimes you find that was the easiest part. Breaking the glass ceiling (more like steel reinforced glass) is another thing all together.

The job market might improve for awhile and then worsen again and then improve again. It's a constant cycle. Then there are the stories about those in middle management who thought they had a stable lifetime job. They were shown the exit door when the profits of the company decreased.

Jobs are being transported to other countries with cheap labor by U.S. companies that make enormous profits. Yet many white people and politicians in the U.S. blame Blacks for taking jobs. They don't seem to notice that the labels on merchandise in stores say made in "China," "Korea" and other countires, the labels don't say made in "South Central, L.A.," "East St. Louis," or "Harlem." They don't notice the Black unemployment rate stays the same or that a white person with a high school diploma can make the same income as a Black person with a college degree. Some one may think you got a job only because of affirmative action and not because of qualifications. They never consider that whites have gotten jobs for centuries simply because they were white, and continue to do so.

BE ALL YOU CAN BE

You know some people are trying to fool you. They pump you up by telling you "Be all you can be." Then when you go out and try to do this, you sometimes get knocked down. Look at how Deion Sanders was treated by the sports announcers and team management, when he tried to play professional baseball and football. Some acted like he had raped their daughters. These hypocrites are probably still telling people, "Be all you can be."

When the press gave rappers a hard time for sampling other artists music, many Black folks jumped on the "I don't like rap" bandwagon. They didn't stop to figure out what was going on and how this criticism was connected to other racial issues. For years whites around the world have been copying Black music and making money. It didn't become a problem until young Black males and females decided to copy Black music and make money off it.

I'm also not against running for political office, but I once heard a rapper say, "363 Black mayors and still no juice."

This is a great time for you to explore other areas of employment and personal fulfillment and get off the cycle. What can you do for the benefit of the community, your country and the global community that will also benefit you? There are many things that are needed in the African-American community that could easily support many businesses. You only have to look at ads in Black magazines and commercials on BET to see what companies are selling to us. They consider our market important. Why can't you?

The global community awaits to respond to the different creative ideas that you can come up with. Music, dance and sports are not the only things that you are talented at. Many of you know this, while too many don't. There are many other choices.

And once you start moving in the right direction and you get there. Don't let happen again what happened in Chapter 8 in the book, *Before The Mayflower, A History of Black America* by Lerone Bennett Jr. After the Civil War, Blacks gained a respectable measure of power in the U.S for a few years. Then this power was taken away by the U.S. government and by people who were allowed by the government to do what evil they pleased upon Black people.

THE MINIMUM WAGE TRAP

Minimum wage is $4.25 an hour. For two weeks that's $340, and a year's pay equals only $8160. After taxes, you have around $7000.

At $6.00 an hour, that's only $11,520 a year-around $9800 a year after taxes. In recent years the working poor has paid a larger percentage of their pay to taxes than the rich. There are millions of people of all races who only make about this much. After paying bills, insurance and other living expenses, often there is not much left. You must be aware of this when planning your future.

I've visited schools that have over a 70% majority of Black students, yet the A and A-B honor roll at these same schools, is over 90% white students. You need to figure out the reason for this and what can you do about it. Does this have something to do with Black poverty and some young Blacks committing crimes?

If only we would stop loving things that don't love us. You're always hurting when you love something that doesn't love you.

FREEDOM STRATEGY #14

WHERE DOES HIGH SELF-ESTEEM COME FROM

Blacks and whites have a tendency to enlarge our faults while not making note of white people's faults. The bad guy these days is the media and it's portrayal of Blacks. But we do our own portraying, too. I've been to many meetings, gatherings and shows that whites controlled, that started late or were poorly organized. I'm sure you have too. Yet Blacks came up with CPT (color people time) for us but nothing negative for others.

What about the deficit, the billion-dollar S & L scandal for which the minority white male crooks did little time in jail? What about government waste, white on white crime, mass murders and serial killers, etc. These were mostly brought about by whites.

What do excess salt and sugar, fat on meat, cigarettes and their smoke, smoke from factories, cocaine and crack, have in common?

They are the color white. But we have not given them a negative "white" name as Black has been used to name things that are bad. You know, the black list. But a news reporter giving the news would never call dying in a blizzard or cancer caused by cigarettes a "white death."

These negative words invented by Americans are used in schools every day. Black and white kids associate the color black with bad things and most transfer this association to people. These children grow into adults. Some have healthy minds, but too many don't. What do you think would happen to white kids bombarded with negative "white" words while in their development years? Would white become less desirable? We already know Black is less desirable. White flight, private schools, opinion polls and a number of other things tell us this.

We even go so far as to make a difference between light skin and dark skin in our own community. We produce our own mental slavery. The reason we do this is pure ignorance and the result is internal self-defeating conflict.

THE REAL WHITE LIE

What if public service commercials started saying, "you're destroying your mind and your body with that white cocaine" or "that white crack." Would this have a positive or negative effect on people. Would it make any difference? Do you think some whites would continue to think they were superior and stop identifying Blacks with bad? Would some misguided Blacks stop identifying Blacks as bad?

I marvel at the elders. How could they develop such a belief in themselves and their Black race when they were so downtrodden. They were forced into the dirt more than most of us will ever be, yet they believed. Far too many of us don't have enough courage to simply believe in ourselves and our race when we have less obstacles than they did.

We've seen many whites on talk shows and in person who supposedly have been showered with positive images to make them proud. Many believe in themselves and have high self-esteem.

Yet many still do not. They join cults, radical religious groups and other clannish organizations to find direction in their lives and to boost their self-esteem. And often are easily led astray. Although not labeled in the press, alcoholism and drug abuse are high in many places in the white community. Groups like the Klan have low beliefs, low self-esteem and often feel they do not measure up to what a supreme white person is suppose to be able to do. It hurts if a Black person is out doing them, especially in mental abilities. Their last hope is to be better than anyone Black. Did all of these people miss the "supreme white self-esteem train," or is there more to it?

The supreme power rests within you. Focus more on how you feel about yourself than how you think white people feel about you. Do not give anyone your power!

FREEDOM STRATEGY #15

TAKING THIS COUNTRY
FOR GRANTED

Foreigners say all the time that Americans take their country for granted. Often foreigners don't have the same freedoms in their country that Americans have. They have few rights and less opportunities to advance themselves or their families.

Then they come to America. We agree that the United States has a lot of problems, but more opportunities than most countries. Once here, the new Americans start businesses and begin to move themselves to a higher economic level. Most of the time, it's not because of gifts or grants, but because of savings, strategy and hard work. They take advantage of the opportunities they see, while those born here remain blind to these same opportunities.

The misconception is that foreigners are given gifts and grants over other people. Sadly some use this as a crutch as to why they have not advanced. Instead of moving up, they play the lifetime victim and stay down. They are secure in the knowledge that others are down also.

There is evil racism. But, if a person keeps planning and working toward a big goal, they can beat racism, or at least operate at a better level. First remove the limitations on your mind. The mental prison.

I once heard a story of how a huge elephant was trained to not run away. Held by a large chain to a post, it tried over and over to break the chain. Finally the elephant gave up and accepted it's fate. The chain could now be removed and replaced by a rope that the elephant could break. But it did not try to break away because the elephant could see that it was still tied. The chain was now in the mind, not on the leg. The trainers didn't have to worry that the elephant would move farther than the small rope would allow.

So it is with far too many African-Americans. Although there is a rope holding us, mostly the chain is on the mind.

Those that have been here all along do not see opportunities. They see only the chains that are keeping them from being successful. This is similar to when a person thinks an object is valuable while you throw it in the thrash. Or, when one person is willing to pay a lot of money for an item, but you would not want it for free.

You do not see the value.

Sometimes you can give a child a very nice toy and they are not excited about it. But let the company that makes the toy spend millions of dollars on flashy TV advertising, and suddenly the child thinks that toy is the best thing in the world and asks for it.

We are like this child, but unlike the toy maker. No one is spending millions of dollars to help us see the value of something, and that something is you. Why should they? You might wake up one day and advance past them.

For 246 years white power held Blacks in slavery and freed us without a nickel.

—Benjamin E. Mays

FREEDOM STRATEGY #16

THE BLACK COLLEGE CAN PROSPER FINANCIALLY

Author's note: Each person should give financial support to Black colleges. Everyone receives benefits from the existence of the Black college.

Most of the best Black athletes go to white colleges. Many white colleges have Black student populations below five percent. But usually 60 percent or more of the atheletes on the football and basketball teams are Black. The Black athlete is the protected and pampered minority. He receives more goodies than the white student body, even when racist incidents increase on white campuses. While some Black students are resented and discriminated against, the Black athlete brings in huge sums of money and prestige. I've even heard of cases where Black athletes were accused of raping white girls and beat the rap. They may get a short suspension for misconduct, but soon they are back in the arena performing. Even the press and fans don't get too upset. Soon the story fades from the newspaper.

Why do they go to white colleges and wear Malcolm X caps (at least while they are in style) instead of going to Black colleges? Then the Black colleges could reap the financial rewards and gain prestige. Certainly it's not because they really think they're going to get a better education. Or the old "halftime show" lie that they are there mostly for an education. Many don't graduate or take fluff courses.

THE BIG QUESTION

Many Blacks consider this country to be racist (or somewhat racist). And believe that racism has been a major factor in denying our progress, past and present. So why do the Black athletes go make millions of dollars for the white schools instead of the Black schools who often struggle financially?

Often the prestige of the white schools is based more on the success of the athletic programs than on academics. Do they really have a better chance at making the pros, a better chance at fame and fortune, better national exposure, get more illegal money under the table, better jobs during and after college, white girls and better drugs?

Hell, the Black colleges could give them all of this, and probably swing the white girls too. (Just a joke, folks) "If Southern University (a Black college) had a few basketball players from the All-American teams, they could blow through the NCAA tournament and make it to the final four. In that final four you suddenly had Jackson State, who had blown through the same as Southern. The same thing could happen in the NIT. Other Black schools could play large white universities and beat them. Wouldn't this be just as good or better?"

The players would still get national exposure, and the star players would still get million dollar contracts.

A HISTORIC EVENT

But the greatest thing is that, for the first time in history, the Black schools could make big money off the Black athlete. Suddenly, many Black schools would be more prestigious than white schools. African-Americans would be wearing jackets, caps, tee-shirts and other merchandise with the name of Black colleges on them instead of glorifying the white university names. This means more money and recognition for Black colleges. These colleges could in turn let the Black community and Black students make this merchandise, thus providing a lifetime of economic education for the students and upliftment of the surrounding communities.

In football the 1993 per team payoff for the Rose Bowl was 6.5 million dollars. While Black colleges try to raise a few thousands dollars each year.

I'LL TRADE YOU SOME SHOES
FOR A MILLION DOLLARS

The coaches at white universities get talk shows, large salaries, free housing and other benefits. One coach received a million dollar shoe contract plus stock options on top of a six figure salary. The players aren't required to wear the shoes, but most do, supposedly because they are free. In a good year, one player gets a professional contract. Some of the Black players say the white coaches treat them like sons. I see why they treat you like a son. But do this, go get a qualified Black person and have them apply for a good paying job on the college campus (without your pull), and see what happens. What likely will happen, is what most Black male ex-athletes will face once they enter the working world.

The coaches are made into legends by the fans and press. Buildings are named after them. This is mostly due to the Black athlete, but this fact doesn't get press. Their program is big time due to the Black athlete, not the other way around. Some win their conference and go to the final four in the NCAA consistently. They only have the greatest talent to work with. Not only do they get the best Black players, but naturally they get the best white players as well.

Have you ever heard of a top white athlete considering going to a majority Black school? They would never consider bringing their talent to a Black school. The Black school then would benefit from the skills of the white athlete. Maybe that would be something like reverse discrimination.

Yet, at the white schools that have Black coaches and good teams, I've noticed they seldom get the top white players. The top white players uses their right to select.

AMOS AND ANDY

Some white colleges have a Black coach or a Black face out front. Blacks choose to like college teams that seem to represent blackness such as Georgetown, UNLV and Michigan (teams unliked by most whites). In the back is where control lies – behind the Black faces. The athletic director and other ruling bodies determine the hiring and firing and what the money is used for. Most often Black students on white campuses have to protest for anything that relates to them. This goes on today. The white university always reminds the Black students that they are a minority when they want something. But it's okay for their majority Black teams to bring in huge sums of money and prestige for the white universities.

The big money that the Black athletes bring in goes to school programs and makes the white university better. Historically they receive more than their share of state and federal money. At least 95% of the money the Black athletes works, toils and sweats for goes to aid the 95% or more white student body (if there are 15,000 students and 3% are Black, that's only 450 Black students). At the same time some Black students have an extra hard time passing courses because the teacher doesn't like Blacks, and the Black students often get notes slid under their dorm door that say "Nigger go home." Campus newspapers frequently publish articles that insult all Blacks.

THE LATEST RODNEY KING OF BASKETBALL; MICHIGAN'S FAB FIVE

The press and the white sports announcers say on a regular basis that Black players are loafing, not thinking or doing something stupid. The same things are not said about the white players. This often is the same in the working world.

While in the arena, the Black and white athletes hug and support each other. The student body cheers and prays for a victory, and the best player, regardless of color, religion, sexual orientation and looks is given a chance to perform and bring in that money and glory. It doesn't matter. It's a true color blind society. Maybe all African-Americans should suit up!

Let these players go to Black colleges. The Black coach suddenly would be the greatest coach in the world, largely because of the Black athletes.

With all that the Black athletes do for white colleges, they receive very little in return. The white schools receive a huge return off a small investment. Under the table money only goes so far. Permanent jobs from boosters have limited futures and often go only to star performers. The proud ex-athelete is now only a welfare dependent. He fades back into the Black community he left.

Because of the abundance of talent and few openings, few college athletes are drafted. There are 324 players in the NBA and only a handful of openings each year. There are around 1800 college seniors playing basketball!

No money goes to the athletes' community, which is often poor. You could write a thick book about the many college athletes that end up with almost no money, no education and no self-respect. Black universities could reverse this trend.

NOT A HELLUVA LOT OF DIFFERENCE

Today is similar to the days of slavery. Back then a robust slave was auctioned off to the highest bidder. This slave made money for the master through labor, battles with other slaves or by reproducing others for slavery. The slave master was the only one to reap financial benefit, not the slaves. It's almost exactly like that today. Only the Black athlete has a choice. We suffer from crippling low self-esteem, the inner belief that we are second and third class citizens. But we feel like first class citizens if we are accepted around whites. We are easily fooled and taken in when some whites decide to treat us like somebody. This is the main reason why Black athletes go to white schools.

Jimmy the Greek said we were bred for "physical benefits." If so not much has changed, because whites receive more benefits from the Black athletes than Blacks do. No wonder the white minority male in power got rid of Jimmy the Greek. While most Blacks weren't offended by the truth (or partial truth), they didn't want someone around to remind us, because we might start thinking about it and make changes.

It's time to break the ancient cycle and past time for Black colleges to be more aggressive and creative in recruiting the best Black athletes. It's worth the effort. The parents and the community of the athletes should be better educated on what is going on and enlisted to help in this effort. The Black athlete is rightfully the sons and daughters of Black colleges, but has been given away or sold for the benefit of others. We have gone along with this tragedy for too long.

NOTE: An excellent article that I recommend to athletes, Black college administrators and anyone interested is an April 93 article in *Worth* magazine entitled 'The Deal Maker — Confessions of an Agent — Sleazy, slimy, double dealing? You may have what it takes.' It can be found in the library or on microfiche.

PART 4—
FREEDOM STRATEGIES

DOING POSITIVES

FREEDOM STRATEGY #17

VOLUNTEER

Volunteer opportunities exists in most towns and cities. They are listed in the newspaper or you can call a company or organization to learn of their volunteer programs. This offers you a chance to contribute to your community, add a positive to your resume, and make contacts within the company. Often volunteer work allows you to meet the top people in a company. Networking with all responsible people is equally important.

FREEDOM STRATEGY #18

ENROLL IN CONTINUING EDUCATION CLASSES FOR EDUCATION AND TO MAKE BUSINESS CONTACTS

In universities and technical schools across the country, you find retirees and established business people going to continuing education classes. Courses range from business and history to art and basketweaving. Pick a class that allows interaction.

These classes have retirees, business owners and people who work for companies that have valuable business contacts. It's an easy way to make valuable business contacts while learning a craft and pursuing more knowledge.

FREEDOM STRATEGY #19

UNEMPLOYED, LOOKING TO MOVE UP OR CHANGE CAREER? ATTEND CONVENTIONS

Conventions have something in common, most everybody there is employed. Conventions are a great place to go and meet people casually when you are looking to switch careers, move up or get a job.

Most people think of conventions as a time to get more knowledge, relax, and socialize. This allows a better way to meet people and make contacts then the formal personnel visit.

Almost every profession has conventions. Local newspapers usually post the dates when a convention is coming to town. The January issue of Black Enterprise magazine has a pullout section that list various conventions. Or, contact an organization or business to find out when and where.

71

FREEDOM STRATEGY #20

SUCCESS THROUGH COMMUNICATIONS

It's important to be able to express your thoughts to others. Whatever is on your mind might be clear to you but once you tell someone, the message becomes unclear.

I've often heard people say they don't have much education or that they aren't college educated before they speak. Some people who have good things to say don't feel confident in expressing themselves and remain quiet. What's worse is people that have nothing to say but talk all the time! Education is not a cure-all. I know people with little education that are very intelligent and have a lot to offer. Yet when I was in college I met some of the most ignorant people I've ever known. It's not always about getting a formal education. You can get an education by just reading and thinking and discuss what you read.

Stating your thoughts to others is something you must do well to be successful. You'll need the encouragement and help of other people to advance in life.

Some of our best speakers are people who were once very shy. They used incorrect English and had trouble expressing themselves. To develop communication skills, enroll in a speaking course at a local college or technical school. Watch speech training shows on a PBS channel and listen to people on television that are well-spoken and repeat whatever they say out loud, or into a tape recorder. We learned to talk as a baby, by repeating what others said.

Practice, and soon you will notice a difference.

FREEDOM STRATEGY #21

A LESSON FROM JESSE

When Jesse Jackson ran for president he said "keep hope alive," "common ground" and "stop exporting jobs." He also said "reinvest in America," "reinvest in education," and "the rich must pay their fair share of taxes." He even talked about doing something for Americans without health insurance." These were all themes and national causes copied by the press and candidate Bill Clinton four years later to get elected. After the inaugural of Bill Clinton, I almost expected the new President to pull off a mask and say, "I kept hope alive."

The network news and newspapers ignored this repeat of Jesse's words and themes that made him a respected presidential candidate. Many saw the truths and wisdom in his words. His opponents and the press however keyed in on his speaking abilities as a way to ignore other positive issues that he talked about.

One lesson here is that a lot of us feel we know what to do for our best interest. There are creative ideas and all kinds of earth-shaking positive changes that are in us waiting to come out. BRING THEM OUT! The difference is, we don't need people to vote us into office first. We are free to take control of our own destiny today. If we choose we can put our big plans into action right away.

The first step is a decision — a determination.

How Jesse was not acknowledged for his ideas and themes is a mirror image of what has happened in America since slavery — the ignoring of contributions. If you feel that you can wait on the government or someone else to acknowledge you or pass a law that will help you, you are not living. The government cannot pass a law that will make you a accepted and respected woman. Only you can do that. Besides, what they give, they can also take away. Don't look for respectability and acceptance in someone else's eyes.

As long as you are doing what's right, your self-respect and happiness should not depend on whether other people accept or like you. They are not gifts that can be given, at least not to an adult.

PART 5—
FREEDOM STRATEGIES

A HIGHER LEVEL

It is idle, a hollow mockery, for us to pray to God to break the oppressor's power, while we neglect the means of knowledge which will give us the ability to break this power. — God will help us when we help ourselves.

—Frederick Douglass

FREEDOM STRATEGY #22

JAMES, 2nd Chapter, 26 verse

Author's note: Across the country, there are some Black church-es and church members tirelessly working together and in-dividually to make a positive impact in our people lives and the future of our country. There are far too many that are not.

For as the body without the spirit is dead,
so faith without works is dead also.

I struggled with using this title more than any other because I can see someone throwing out Bible verses to support how they feel, while ignoring the real issues.

For as the body without the spirit is dead, so faith without works is dead also. Do you consider yourself a spiritual person

81

who believes in GOD, or a person that have spiritual faith but does not believe in any particular religion?

Either way, if you are not working every day to improve yourself, your family and your community, then your faith is dead. It's not there. It's a fake, a sham, a lie.

How can you claim to believe in something great and have faith that everything will work out if you are not doing anything to make a positive difference in your life and the life of others? Not only in small ways but also in big ways. To have faith means you believe in something that is great. It does not mean small acts or narrow-minded thinking.

No one is going to appear any time soon and fix everything with a wave of their hand. Do we as a people plan to keep suffering until that happens, and then after we are gone our children can continue the traditional suffering, and then their children?

WAITING FOR CHANGE

Currently what is preached in most Black churches is that the person should pray to cope with life's misfortunes instead of having the courage to change them. "Everything will be alright in heaven." The people stay unaware, placid and complacent while outside the door, everything slowly goes to hell.

I've never been able to understand how grown people that see and hear of Black children being killed on the streets, allow the importation of drugs that destroy their children and community. They allow the evils of racism to strangle another generation and other social ills, and do nothing on a large scale to stop it. How can these people think they will be rewarded with an invitation to heaven? Do they really think their spirit will be in heaven talking about how bad things are on earth and saying "what a shame, but I made it out."

There are churches working to make a difference. A great difference is needed, a great faith. We can not meet the many things that are against us with a small effort. It won't work. It might make those who give the effort feel good, but nothing will get better. We have grown too accustomed to the demise of our people, similar to people in California who say they are used to earthquakes. Black folks can't afford to wait.

THE COMFORT ZONE

Talk about the comfort level, the seats in some churches are padded to make you comfortable, your stay there nice. Directly addressing the problems that face African-Americans and putting together a coalition of churches for action would take too much effort and sacrifice. Maybe a Sunday could be spent planning instead of the traditional service (you can still take up collections). These efforts might move the congregation out of it's comfortable position and into direct contact with reality.

One Sunday I was listening to a sermon similar to those I've heard all my life. The previous Friday night there had been a drive by shooting, Black people were injured. This drive by was not a usual thing to happen in this community, yet the pastor never mentioned it in his sermon. No attempt was made to talk about why this and other bad things were happening or what can we do.

Most churches continue to use mostly white labor to build their churches and buildings. It's disturbing to watch mostly white labor building a church and while a few blocks away you see brothers on the corner. And some aren't there because they want to be.

Most churches deposit their money in white-owned banks. Often these are huge sums collected over many years from middle and low income people. Many of them often can't get a loan from the same bank. Although Black banks aren't located in many Black communities. There's no law that says you have to deposit your money locally. With electronic transfer, money can be transfered anywhere in only minutes. Smaller sums can be kept locally for normal operations.

THE COMFORTABLE HABIT

Getting dressed every Sunday morning, going through the same steps you've done all of your life and going to church is the easiest thing to do. It's a habit, a very comfortable habit. When people that go to church every Sunday miss a Sunday, they get that feeling that something was missing from their day. The rest of the week just doesn't seem right.

It's not the spiritual fulfillment their missing. If that was so, after a life of receiving spirituality on top of spirituality they would be out trying to bring a positive impact to their race in their great time of need.

No, it's not the spirituality that was missed. It was the habit. Sometimes it seems people go to church to be entertained.

We are told to be Christ-like. Jesus left his family at an early age and went out to meet the many needs of the people. He was not a sit-around savior. He took salvation to the people.

MEETING THE NEEDS OF THE PEOPLE

When you visit many Black Churches they have few if any young Black males between the ages of 15 and 30. Why is this? It's the same reason you go shop at a certain store. There's something there that is meeting your needs. You are being serviced. The young Black male is not in church because his needs are not being met and the churches refuse to be creative on a large scale in meeting these needs. Part of their foundation crumbles away as a result.

If you had a tape of a sermon you heard as a child and compared it to a sermon you heard recently, it would be the same. About having faith, believing. The big difference is that Black America did not have some of the major concerns of today along with some past concerns. We are at a cross roads, a historical place in history.

Today leaders need to communicate in a fashion that young men and women can easily understand and relate to without question. I don't mean give a rap-inspired sermon, but sadly many church leaders today are narrowly focused. While many young African-American men and women drown in a sea of hopelessness, the church refuses to use creative solutions on a large scale. They continue to build houses of Babylon.

Whenever I see the movie The Ten Commandments, I know most Black people weren't with Moses when he parted the Red Sea to escape Pharaoh's soldiers. Many of us would not have gone through. We would have held hands and started singing "We Shall Overcome" while Pharaoh's soldiers were coming to destroy us. This is where we are today, the soldiers today are our many social ills. To be saved we have to go through to the other side.

FREEDOM STRATEGY #23

ONE THING THE BLACK CHURCH CAN DO

Here is an idea so powerful that if enacted, it will have amazing results. Since eating is one of the things they say people will always do, the Black churches in each city or town could unite and open a supermarket. Of course this idea will fit some places better than others. If this is not ideal for your location, come up with other ideas. I've read and heard many times of money being raised to build a church or retire a mortgage. Churches could come together and buy a large, suitably located building, then have an elected ruling body composed of each church. Make this the cleanest, the friendliest, best managed, best priced and most profitable supermarket around.

THE BENEFITS

1. A built in market. Church members would shop there and also encourage others. Each person could tell many other people. Supporting the community will also encourage others to shop there.

2. Provides employment and training for Black youth.

3. Many of the products the supermarket sells can be made locally by the Black community. A small business can be created and easily supported by the steady sale of canned goods, frozen goods, snacks, cleaning supplies, etc. Once again this will provide employment, self-dependency and high self-esteem.

4. People will get other ideas on what they can do and do it.

5. The success of this venture will translate into political and economic power.

6. There will be less concern with racism and more concern with improving people and the community.

7. The church will see a substantial increase in contributions.

PART 6—
FREEDOM STRATEGIES

TAKE IT TO THE
NEXT LEVEL

FREEDOM STRATEGY #24

PATTERN YOURSELF AFTER ANY PERSON, ANY RACE

I'm reminded of those women who told me that they would have to see an example of someone just like them in my book who has succeeded before they would believe they can lift themselves to a better life.

I remembered reading many articles and seeing programs of people just like them who were making it in a big way. They knew of these things, so I figured there must be more to it than what they said.

When I say "pattern yourself," I don't mean fashion, physical appearances, mannerisms and so on.

91

If you need an example of a successful person to use as a guide to your own success, you don't have to find someone of the same sex or race. This is very limiting and it's one of the foundations of low self-esteem and small thinking. The myth that a Black woman can only do what another Black woman is already doing is a holdover from slavery and repression. And it's now self-repression.

The myth is that one must find another successful African-American female as a role model or mentor when they wish to copy the success of someone. This is not true.

We are the only race that has been taught this great lie and continue to believe it and teach it to ourselves. Japan would be a poor country if they held this belief. Many of the products they now make billions from were first developed in the United States. They simply copied and improved on these products. Then they surpassed the U.S in many areas. Not many people in America resemble Japanese.

Feel free to pattern yourself after anyone (even people you don't like) or any business. We all know others have patterned many things after Africans both in Africa and America, and profited from it. No thank you or acknowledgement has ever been given.

Now it's your time. Simply believe that you can do what any other person is doing, because you can.

FREEDOM STRATEGY #25

WHITE MEN CAN'T JUMP,
also known as
BLACK PEOPLE CAN'T THINK

How many times after seeing ads for the movie 'WHITE MEN CAN'T JUMP' do you think a lot of white people thought to themselves, or said out loud "maybe I can't jump high but at least I can think. I'll take being able to think to being able to jump high any time."

On an Oprah Winfrey show entitled 'WHY WHITE MEN FEAR BLACK MEN' based on the November 1992 Essence magazine, a Black man said that white men fear Blacks will take over in business areas the same way they have taken over in professional sports. Football and basketball were once white male dominated sports.

A white male replied "you can have the sports, we will take the business and thinking areas." This white male appeared

93

on a later show and said that people had told him that they agreed with him. What he said is how a lot of white people feel.

Most of us agree that a lot of white people think we are mentally deficient. The rest can read Part One of the book *Two Nations — Black and White, Separate, Hostile, Unequal* by Andrew Hacker. We also heard this point of view from the Germans under Hitler's rule. Recently the Japanese have said the same things about Blacks in America. The Japanese have said on several occasions that we were deep in debt, and have low abilities. They said that we are lazy and unproductive in business, we are the cause of America's economic problems. This received great attention in the national news over and over. What about the Koreans, the Chinese and other races around the world? Is this a global point of view? Is this point of view based on racism?

In my opinion, the white male on Oprah was saying that Blacks excel at sports but not in business and thinking. We are strong in the limbs but weak in the brain. Blacks who think are an exception to the rule. Like twins being born, it happens every now and then. What do you think other races form their opinions on?

First, let's assume this white male isn't a racist or wasn't brought up to feel the way he does. Assume that his opinions were based on things that he had heard or seen.

Did he form an opinion when he heard what the Japanese said about Blacks? Did he then see Blacks driving new Japanese cars knowing that the Japanese hire few Blacks and locate their U.S. plants far from where Blacks live? Did he hear of more young Blacks dying at each other's hands today then died during the Vietnam war. Did he think they call white people racist but murder each other?

When he heard about Black entertainers coming from poverty, making it big, ending up broke, bankrupt or on drugs and never doing anything big for the poor communities they come from, and he formed an opinion?

Did he form an opinion when he heard that many businesses in the inner cities are owned by Koreans or whites? Blacks complain about how these whites and Koreans discriminate against them or don't respect them. Yet the stores make a good profit off of Black customers.

Did he read that money from Blacks accounts for 23 percent of the billion dollar shoe market. Yet Blacks represent less than an estimated 3 percent of the professional work force in the shoe market. At the same time, Black unemployment is twice that of whites. Black athletes sell the shoes on television and are well paid. But obviously they do not have any great influence on hiring.

Black kids kill each other over these shoes and jackets. Poor and middle class Black parents go out to buy shoes or other products from a company that will not hire them or their child. What about cosmetics, toy makers and many other industries? They advertise to the Black community, but they do not hire more than a token number of Blacks. Do you think other races form opinions when they know that we support these companies with our hard earned money?

On the other hand, let's assume that this man is a racist and will always be one and that one hundred percent of his views are based on a racist point of view and nothing else. Do you feel better with this point of view-more comfortable at least?

I believe African-Americans come from great people and today as a race we have the potential to achieve greatness. That potential is very possible to realize.

At this moment, then, the Negroes must begin to do the very thing which they have been taught that they cannot do. They still have some money, and they have needs to supply. They must begin immediately to pool their earnings and organize industries to participate in supplying social and economic demands. If the Negroes are to remain forever removed from the producing atmosphere, and the present discrimination continues, there will be nothing left for them to do.

—Carter G. Woodson

I believe in Black power as long as it demonstrates to Black people that our power comes from unity, and that political and economic power can never be achieved by fighting among ourselves.

—Benjamin E. Mays

FREEDOM STRATEGY #26

YOU HAVE ALWAYS ENTERTAINED US; FOR THE BLACK ATHLETE/ENTERTAINER

Author's note: If Black entertainers decided to individually or unite with the goal of making economic changes in the Black community they would make a positive historic impact.

I know that most people will think I'm focusing on those Black entertainers that are well known. This applies as much to those who aren't as well known and those retired from their respective fields. They far outnumber the familiar names.

Andrew Hacker, a white male, wrote *Two Nations, Black and White, Separate, Hostile, Unequal.* A statement was made to Mr. Hacker by a Black person in an audience, "with all the advances Blacks have made in sports and entertainment, some of the top people in those fields, why did white America still see us as inferior?"

He replied, "You have always entertained us."

Most Black entertainers have never transcended performing. The exceptions are rare. Most (not all), of the exceptions have not tried to help those in need in any major way. This sad fact dates back to slavery.

The strong slave competed in brutal contests with other Black slaves. The slave's master profited and his status and ego increased with winning contests. This hero slave had a special status with other slaves on the plantation and extra benefits including the gratitude, admiration and care from his master and other whites, sometimes to the point of respect and love. They could love him because of his superior physical abilities. The lot of the hero slave improved as long as he kept winning. The lot of the other slaves stayed the same.

Status was given to the slave as long as he kept his place. He was only to use his mind to figure out strategies to beat an opponent. His strategy was second to the master's strategy or another white man. He was great and strong but not a white man, nor had he the choice of a white man to make decisions and chart his own course in life. He was still a slave. His self-esteem was only allowed to go so far. He could not transcend his contests.

Today's entertainers have a chance to go to the next level. But do not; they feel it's not in their best interest, are afraid, don't care, they don't see any major problems, don't have the knowledge or think they can acquire the knowledge.

THE SILENT MAJORITY

I believe that Al Campanis and Marge Schott based some of what they said about Black athletes on what they see and hear. They have to wonder why some entertainers don't come to the aid of their people. They hear about the poverty and unemployment rate of Black youth (which many people believe has a lot to do with the crimes and killings taking place). They hear about the complaints of discrimination in the workforce. On the other hand they must notice the white agents, lawyers and managers many Black athletes hire. They must think that Black athletes believe what Al Campanis said, that "Blacks don't have the necessary qualities."

Some people could easily finance many businesses by the money that is spent on excessive materialism (thinking big only when it comes to building houses) or wasted by mismanagement, mostly by white management. Take the criticism of Don King. Maybe he is a crook, maybe he isn't. But one thing is for sure, for every Black agent that has mismanaged or stole an athlete's money. There have been far more white agents guilty of the same thing. But I haven't seen any television shows about the rip-off of Black athletes by their white agents and managers. I have seen shows about Don King.

Around the country many single Black women with children work every day (some with two jobs) but are barely getting by, which is the same situations many Black athletes come from. Often these women could receive more benefits if they quit their jobs and went on welfare. A welfare system promoted by society and allowed by us.

It's revealing to read articles written about white males who are heads of corporations and they say "that role models and mentors made a difference and continues to have a positive impact on their lives." With all the advantages they had and being where they are from. Someone reaching back to them still made a big difference. Yet for the Black children in dire straits no one wants that responsibility. Being responsible is too much trouble is how some people feel. People do not want entertainers to raise their kids, but would like for people to be caring and aware and show those feelings through their actions.

THE NEXT LEVEL

What if the entertainers decided to seek out talented African Americans in the business arena with the intention of investing in the Black community? (Not those in the business arena who aren't concern about nobody but themselves and their families.) Not in a small thinking way, but on a grand scale. The same thinking scale the owners of teams used when they bought the teams or when a studio invests in a large budget movie.

Any business idea should include ways where those that benefit could produce and sell a product to cover all costs. So what is needed as much as money is creative interests.

THE OLD AND NEW REALITIES ARE THE SAME

African Americans have been under the mistaken notion that if we excel in allowable areas, entertainment/sports, respect and admiration would transfer to the business arena. Doors that were closed would swing wide open with opportunity.

We celebrated our atheletes and worshipped movie stars and singers, felt proud they are the top in their respective fields and thought this would make a difference for all African-Americans. Everyone could see how skillful and talented we were. Don't whites love it when we thrill them, sing and dance like nobody else, make them laugh, perform feats requiring superhuman physical skills. Don't they worship the performers, buy the products they advertise and some will fight another white person for your sake, and the team sake. You're fantastic, they love you. Surely this will make a difference in racial relations and open doors for other Blacks outside the arena.

Then and now. "You have always entertained us."

If there is no struggle there is no progress. Those who profess to favor freedom and yet deprecate agitation, are men who want crops without plowing up the ground, they want rain without thunder and lightning. They want the oceans without the awful roar of it's many waters.

This struggle may be a moral one, or it may be a physical one, or it may be both moral and physical, but it must be a struggle. Power concedes nothing without a demand. It never did and it never will----Men may not get all they pay for in this world, but they must certainly pay for all they get.

—Frederick Douglass

FREEDOM STRATEGY #27

BECOME AN ACTIVIST

You can bring about changes in your life and the lives of others by getting involved locally and nationally. You can make a change by being active.

What is there to get involved in, you ask? Wherever you see a need to change something or a need to inform people, to bring about social or economic change. Do it yourself or form a group to help. Or you can join an existing activist group. Don't wait for someone to take action or sit around saying "something needs to be done." Normally when people say that, they mean someone else needs to take action. The problem continues to go on and never seems to right itself. The old generation fades away and the new generation is faced with the same problems. We would be better off by taking control of the situations (social ills) in our communities. The results of them controlling us are obvious.

SOME THINGS TO BE AWARE OF WHEN YOU BECOME AN ACTIVIST
(Some apply to daily life)

1. YOUR OWN PREPAREDNESS

Be ready before you go out. Educate yourself. Know the issues so that you may stay focused and not get distracted from the main cause.

Don't try to do everything on your own. There are many good, concerned people to help. Don't fear failure, fear not trying.

2. REQUIRING THANKS

It's only human and right to want to be acknowledged for your good works. But, it can become crippling to the cause when receiving thanks or recognition becomes required. It's even worse when it's expected and thanks never comes. Remember what Langston Hughes said, "We build temples for tomorrow, strong as we know how, and we stand on top of the mountain, free within ourselves."

3. ON THE SURFACE AGREEMENT

You will meet many who agree with you and your cause. But as soon as you stumble and are cut and bleeding, like sharks they rush in for the kill. I've seen a version of this in newspaper columnists who were sort of outraged about the Rodney King beating and outcome of the first trial. Later they really became outraged when the policemen were retried. They then felt that the policemen would not receive a fair trial and were innocent.

4. BEING TYPECAST

Some will try to put you in a category as a way to identify you and as a means to control you. Any success you achieve, they may try to take away. The term "Liberal" is used by politicians as a means to send racial messages to white voters and to control what their other opponents do and say. In reality, most humans are too complex to be defined so narrowly. If you choose to be defined, define yourself. Don't let others do it.

5. INSIDE JEALOUSY AND ENVY

Sadly, this often occurs if you are successful at your efforts. We should fight these evil feelings with all our might.

Those close to you will play on your emotions, or threaten to abandon you when you need them most. Some will kiss you on the cheek and then point you out to your enemies. You will have to do battle in the world and then at home. Those you expect to be happy for you may be "sort of happy." They may expect something from you and try to put guilt trips on you.

Any success will mean to some people that you've changed. In reality they have changed towards you. Some will feel a need to put you down by grandstanding. This boosts their self-esteem. Often the people that give you the hardest time when you are successful will bring flowers when you are down and wish you luck. Because you are down, they mean it.

Some will seek to control you through your love for them. "It's for your sake," they will say.

These warnings might not happen, but you must be aware and watchful. If you aren't, you might be shocked. If you know that they might happen, it won't bother you nearly as much and maybe not at all.

Also, hopefully you're not the one that does these things.

6. THEM YESSAR BOSSES

Have you ever noticed that when whites in power are in conflict with Blacks, they find another Black person and put this person against the ones they are having trouble with? When a company is being questioned by the media about a racial issue, they put Black employees out front to answer questions? This is when they consider this Black person the most valuable.

The minority white power structure does this for a number of reasons:

A. Because it has worked many times.

B. If they have a Black person that agrees with them, then what the others say must not be true. They expect everyone to see it that way.

C. Since some whites believe we all think the same. They will believe the above.

D. Divide and conquer still works.

E. The only time a Black person's words carry much weight is when it is being used against another Black person to uphold the power structure. This is true in the court room as well as the board room. Most often the Black person being used is aware of this also.

F. Someone can always be bought off cheaply. The personal fortune of those being used increases. They get a better job, a raise and what appears to be more respect and admiration from their white associates. They really think of him or her as something less than a man or woman. They know this person is a puppet and a double-crosser.

   During slavery, sometimes other slaves would inform on those who were planning to run away or revolt against the slave masters. Don't be sad or sit and wonder why some Blacks are this weak minded. Defects exists in every race, but we can't afford these people.

   Also, remember that another Black person can have an opposite opinion from you and not be a puppet of the power structure. They should be respected. Use good judgement. But, if you're sure the "YESSAR BOSS STRATEGY" is being used against you, define it for what it is so that others will know.

   Malcolm X had to struggle with this problem. Many that revere him today would have been speaking against him if they were around when he was alive. Martin Luther King also had this problem early on in the Civil Rights struggle. Every African-American's personal creed should be—"I May not be able to help you, but I'm sure as hell not going to hurt you." Even though you may disagree with their methods.

7. THE MEDIA

Even white males in power don't like the media. For you the media can be a handy tool if used properly. Remember the media are people with many of the same concerns and problems that you have. They also have to deal with what life brings.

They also can be deceitful. In an April 1993 article entitled "RACE" in Atlanta magazine, a white male copy editor said, "Being part of the structure that is most responsible for releasing information on race, and seeing the spins that are put on it . . .it's sickening. If people could step into my shoes and see from the inside out how they are manipulated and how we manipulate them on issues of race, it would be a real eye-opener."

You must not totally depend on others to get your message across. Define your position through your own means. The old ways that still work are letters, circulars, posters, newsletters, ads and articles in Black magazines.

Have you ever wondered how a new dance or hip expression found it's way across Black America before getting on the radio or T.V.? Through word of mouth. People can transport ideas. Get your words out.

8. LACK OF SUPPORT

The television show Brooklyn Bridge was canceled by CBS because of low ratings. A grass roots campaign was started by viewers who wanted the show back on television. They got together 6000 signatures, and presented them to CBS. Now the show is to be brought back in another time slot. If it does well it will stay on.

Why did CBS decide to give the show another chance? Because these people let them know that they were interested. Also, what if these 6000 people told all their friends to tell all their friends to boycott the products advertised on CBS and to write and call those advertisers. Losing money certainly would have got their attention.

Often, revenue above everything else is what they believe in. The love of money and power. Using this knowledge means power.

In most cities, you could stand outside nightclubs and get a huge amount of signatures on one weekend.

African-Americans represent the profit margin for a lot of businesses in the U.S., yet discrimination still exists (We represented the profit margin in slavery, too). A lot of places don't hire Blacks some only hire a token few (you know the story). Even businesses that don't depend on Blacks for profit would be affected if we decided to stop buying a certain product, because most everything is connected one way or another. There is no better time than now to take action.

How many times have you heard someone say they wish things would change, but do nothing about it. No army is needed to bring about change, only a well defined strategy and a few good people to carry it out.

9. YOUR OWN NEW POWER

It's the movement that should be celebrated and believed in, much more than the leader of the cause. When the leader enters a room, it's the movement that is being applauded. The name of the movement should be shouted out, not the leader's. Leaders are only human and susceptible to faults.

Leaders are investigated, hounded, and sometimes they just get tired.

A movement that will be strong and has a great chance for success will falter when the people believe more in the leader than the cause. If the leader is caught in a scandal, becomes ineffective or dies, the people will become confused and unfocused. Eventually the great cause is no more. It dies or becomes the living dead.

Many Black men and women have become lost in a wilderness of separate tribes and villages. We are separated by a common language, separated by common problems, and separated by common needs.

People wish every day that Martin Luther King Jr., Malcolm X and other leaders were alive or that someone would come forth and lead them, with the notion that they would lead us to a better day. Like hypocrites we talk of their glory and sing praises to them while not finishing the great things that they started. We wait for a great leader to float down from the sky one day and comfort ourselves in the meantime with the false belief that we are fighting a good fight.

The power and greatness is in the movement, not the person. People die, the cause should live on.

White America cannot save itself if it prevents us from being saved. But, in the nature of things. White America is not going to yield what rightfully belongs to us without a struggle kept up by us. In that struggle our watchword needs to be "work, work, work!" and our rallying cry, "Fight, fight, fight!"

—James Weldon Johnson

FREEDOM STRATEGY #28

(EXCERPT) THE ART OF WAR

The Art of War is a book used by CEOs of billion dollar corporations and many wealthy business people and politicians.

It is one of the best known books of strategy in the world today. *The Art of War* applies to competition and conflict in general on every level. It's aim is invincibility, victory without battle, and strength through understanding of the physics, politics, and psychology of conflict. This is a book that the Black woman can use in business and in their daily life.

Following are a few passages from *The Art of War* and how it applies to African Americans. We are in a war. I will list some ways in which it applys. You can think of many others.

From *The Art of War* by Sun Tzu, translated by Thomas Cleary, Copyrighted 1988 by Thomas Cleary. Reprinted by arrangement with Shambhala Publications, Inc. 300 Massachusetts Avenue, Boston MA 02115.

MASTER SUN

So it is said that if you know others and know yourself, you will not be imperiled in a hundred battles; if you do not know others but know yourself, you win one and lose one; if you do not know others and do not know yourself, you will be imperiled in every single battle.

HAWKINS (Author)

For Black women it is imperative that they believe in themselves and the power that is within them. It is mostly untapped and waiting to be used. This power must be understood and used. The same strength that our ancestors used to endure years of slavery exists today in every Black woman. Get to know that power and use it for worthy pursuits. Learn what you will be up against—have a plan.

MASTER SUN

In ancient times skillful warriors first made themselves invincible, and then watched for vulnerability in their opponents.

HAWKINS

First prepare yourself, learn from your mistakes and those of others. Educate yourself and become more aware. Then, go out.

MASTER SUN

So you should take away the energy of their armies, and take away the heart of their generals.

ZHANG YU

Energy is what battle depends on. Any living thing can be stirred to fight, but even those who fight without regard for death are the way they are because their energy compels them to be that way. Therefore the rule for military operations is that if you can stir up the soldiers of all ranks with a common anger, then no one can stand up to them. Therefore, when opponents first come and their energy is keen, you break this down by not fighting with them for the time being. Watch for when they slump into boredom, then strike, and their keen energy can be taken away.

As for taking away the heart of their generals, the heart is the ruler of the general—order and disorder, courage and timidity, all are based on the mind. So those skilled in controlling opponents stir into disorder, incite them to confusion, press them into fear—thus can the schemes in their hearts be taken away.

HAWKINS

This strategy is used against African Americans with almost perfect results. When blacks get upset about something, they protest bitterly. Then they stop and get complacent when they think change is coming. A committee is formed to study things and very little changes.

This strategy was used against freed slaves, they hoped for better times. This strategy is also being used today. The schemes in the hearts of freed slaves are also in the hearts of African-Americans today. Another dream deferred. Instead of maintaining what we should already have, we are still trying to acquire.

MASTER SUN

A surrounded army must be given a way out.

DU MU

Show them a way to life so that they will not be in the mood to fight to the death, and then you can take advantage of this to strike them.

HAWKINS

Some are allowed to advance, but it's just enough to pacify us. Those in control know if no one were allowed to advance, a great uprising would occur, and that would be more costly. A little of the pie keeps us from risking that little piece, while our power is given (or taken) away.

MASTER SUN

Do not press a desperate enemy.

ZHANG YU

If the opponents burn their boats, destroy their cooking pots, and come to fight it out once and for all, don't press them, for when animals are desperate they thrash about wildly.

HAWKINS

If African-Americans were to come together and protest through economic and political means while demanding seed monies to start businesses in the inner cities. We would win. Blacks protested in this way during the Civil Rights Movement, and won. The U.S. has given land and money to whites

and continues to give billions to other countries, that have
not contributed to America as much as African-Americans have.

MASTER SUN

Take care of physical health and stay where there are plenty of resources. When there is no sickness in the army, it
is said to be invincible.

HAWKINS

Too many of us are being subdued by excessive alcohol
and drugs. This keeps us complacent and too mentally sick
for any battle. Don't destroy your mind and body with alcohol,
drugs and other harmful elements. Stay healthful and prepared
for your life's battle.

MASTER SUN

In military matters it is not necessarily beneficial to have
more strength, only to avoid acting aggressively; it is enough
to consolidate your power, assess opponents, and get people,
that is all.

CHEN HAO

When your military power is not greater than that of the
enemy, and there is no advantage to move on, it is not necessary
to ask for troops from other countries, just to consolidate your
power and get people among the local workers — then you can
still defeat the enemy.

JIA LIN

A large group striking a small group is not held in high esteem; what is held in high esteem is when a small group can strike a large group.

HAWKINS

To make a difference in America does not take everyone. Don't wait for that glorious day. A focused, determined and self-supporting group with a well thought out plan can make a big difference.

MASTER SUN

The individualist without strategy who takes opponents lightly will inevitably become the captive of others.

HAWKINS

Have goals and a strategy. Or else life is up or down, as others wish. They decide whether you're up in the clouds this year or down in the dirt. If they wake up in the morning and decide you are down, then you are down. Much of the Black community are evidence of no strategy.

DU MU

If they have valuable possessions, soldiers may become attached to them and lack the spirit to fight to the death, and all are pledged to die.

HAWKINS

Some people have good jobs and material possessions. Many of these people are complacent and don't support their race in any great way. They might occassionally speak out against injustices, but many have their heads in the sand. They are afraid of losing their material gains if they stand up.

DU MU

Not until soldiers are surrounded do they each have the determination to resist the enemy and sustain victory. When they are desperate, they put up a united defense.

HAWKINS

When African Americans say "we can not let our race corrode away," we will then unite and depend on ourselves. Will this be too late? If it is, both the weak and the strong will be defenseless.

When David Duke ran for governor of Louisiana, Blacks in Louisiana suddenly felt surrounded by a common enemy. They voted in record numbers. Such a display of power needs to be used all the time in politics and economics. These are desperate times, but it's apparently not desperate enough for most people.

MASTER SUN

Cause division among them.

CAO CAO

Send interlopers to cause rifts among them.

LI QUAN

Break up their accords, cause division between the leadership and their ministers, and then attack.

DU MU

This means that if there are good relations between the enemy leadership and its followers, then you should use bribes to cause division.

CHEN HAO

If they are stingy, you be generous; if they are harsh, you be lenient. That way their leadership and followers will be suspicious of each other, and you can cause division between them.

DU YOU

Seduce them with the prospect of gain, send interlopers in among them, have rhetoricians use fast talk to ingratiate themselves with their leaders and followers, and divide up their organization and power.

ZHANG YU

You may cause rifts between the leadership and their followers, or between them and their allies — cause division, and then take aim at them.

HAWKINS

These strategies have been used many times with effective results against us.

PART 7—
FREEDOM STRATEGIES

LOOKING BEYOND NOW

FREEDOM STRATEGY #29

RECOMMENDED READING

I recommend these books for anyone interested in gaining more knowledge and improving their life. They can be purchased at the book store or checked out at the library. It is always good to have your own copy of a book for reference and to reread the parts that informed or inspired you most. Remember, this is a life time journey, not a temporary visit. The main objective is that you get the knowledge.

1. *The Art of War*, translated by Thomas Cleary.

2. *Succeeding Against The Odds*, John H. Johnson, publisher of Ebony, Jet and Ebony Man. (Part of Mr. Johnson success comes from thinking that Blacks wanted and needed to read about themselves and servicing that need.)

3. *Before the Mayflower – A History of Black America* – Lerone Bennett Jr.

4. *Black Economics-Solutions for Economic and Community Empowerment,* Jawanza Kunjufu, 1-800-552-1991.

5. *Black Enterprise, Emerge, Entrepreneur, Essence* and *Money* magazines.

6. *The Black Women's Guide To Financial Independence* – Cheryl D. Broussard

7. *Live Your Dreams* – Les Brown

8. A good show for everyone but especially for teens is "Teen Summit" on BET and the magazine *YSB* (Young Sisters and Brothers).

9. Any book, magazine or person that inspires you.

Our people have made the mistake of confusing the methods with the objectives. As long as we agree on objectives, we should never fall out with each other just because we believe in different methods or tactics or strategy to reach a common objective. We have to keep in mind at all times that we are not fighting for integration, nor are we fighting for separation. We are fighting for recognition as free humans in this society.

—Malcolm X

FREEDOM STRATEGY #30

THE REACTIONARY RESPONSE VERSUS THE LONG TERM RESPONSE

The Los Angeles riots were a reaction in response to negative actions that had taken place. (The same as the other riots in our past) This reactionary response got positive results from the government. The only problem was, this was a temporary response. After the riots, the Presidential candidates toured the burned out areas and promised substantial action. Before he left office, George Bush vetoed a bill that would have given money to the inner cities. The riots and what caused them was rarely mentioned in the presidential debates a few weeks later. Continuing stories became only paragraphs in the newspaper.

The issues that the riots brought about were not a priority to most people as the months passed. This was the temporary response that had brought temporary results. Buildings are still burnt rubble. Insurance companies canceled policies because they didn't believe things would get better. The gangs are still there and so are the reasons that some people join gangs. The racism and discrimination that slowed down for a little while, is back up to speed, and many places it never paused.

Everything is much the same as before the riots.

A violent reactionary force uses rage, anger and hopelessness that has already been boiling inside the mind and body. Instead of striking out at each other, the not guilty verdicts gave people something more deserving of their hate to strike out at. But riots only lasts so long.

In the meantime rage, anger and hopelessness exist. Slowly, relentlessly and without mercy they burn away our mind and body and destroy our promise.

Instead of the reactionary response, you desire a permanent response, you must take action or we will never be totally free, and forever be the partial slaves.

END / BEGINNING

—DOING MY PART ORGANIZATION—
(The DMP)

For those persons interested in taking a positive active role in addressing political, social and economic issues, this is your opportunity. Together we shall address national issues which are important to us.

WHAT WE WILL DO

1. Let politicans know how we feel about issues important to us.
2. Let U.S. and foreign companies know what we think.
3. Address issues of great national concern.

HOW WILL WE DO THIS

1. Letters, postcards and phone calls.
2. Selective voting.
3. If necessary, boycotting a company or product.

WHAT DO YOU DO NOW

1. Follow directions exactly.
2. Send a short letter about one national issue you wish to address and why. State facts, not what you think. Limit to 5 lines. (List phone number and give permission to give it to a local contact person.) Whatever the most people think is important is where we will start. No more than one or two issues at a time will be addressed.
3. In your letter, enclose a SASE, (a envelope that is already stamped and addressed to yourself), so that we can mail it back to you with the plan. This will cut costs.
4. For less than seventy cents and fifteen minutes, you have begun to take action.

WHAT ELSE IS NEEDED

1. Persons in each town or city to volunteer as local contact persons. Repsonsibility will be keeping no more than twenty local people up to date. State if you're interested in your letter.
2. Self motivated, efficient students at a Black college who can organize a headquarters, run a tight ship and volunteer their services. You will be responsible for handling incoming and outgoing mail, keeping contact people up to date, talking to the press, and other occurring needs. I will pay related costs.

SEND LETTER AND SASE TO:
Future Vision Publishers
Doing My Part Organization
P.O. Box 1195
Asheville, NC 28802

Note: Remember, let's keep this easy and focused.

ORDER FORM – For additional copies for family and friends
Future Vision Publisher P.O. Box 1195 Asheville, N.C. 28802

Cut out with scissors

Please send the following books:

_____# OF COPIES: HOW THE BLACK WOMAN CAN BEGIN TO ACHIEVE FINANCIAL FREEDOM

_____# OF COPIES: HOW THE BLACK MAN CAN BEGIN TO ACHIEVE FINANCIAL FREEDOM

Name: _____

Address _____

City _____ State_____ Zip_____

Price: $12.95 each

Sales tax: North Carolina residents add 78 cents.
Shipping: $2.00 for first book and $1.50 for each additional book

Payment: Check _____ Money order _____

A great opportunity to earn extra money is by selling this book to others as an independent seller. Information on how to market and sell the books is included.
For information write to:
Future Vision Publishers
Sales Information
P.O. Box 1195
Asheville, N.C. 28802